I0821770

barangay

Also by Adrian De Leon

Rouge

barangay

an offshore poem

Adrian De Leon

Photographs by Jason Edward Pagaduan

A Buckrider Book

Published by Buckrider Books
an imprint of Wolsak and Wynn Publishers
280 James Street North
Hamilton, ON L8R2L3
www.wolsakandwynn.ca

Editor for Buckrider Books: Paul Vermeersch | Editor: Canisia Lubrin
Copy editor: Ashley Hisson
Cover and interior design: Sarah Lacasse
Interior photos: Jason Edward Pagaduan
Author photograph: Dylan J. Locke
Typeset in: Arno Pro, Courier
Printed by Coach House Printing Company, Toronto, Canada

10 9 8 7 6 5 4 3 2 1

The publisher gratefully acknowledges the support of the Ontario Arts Council, the Canada Council for the Arts and the Government of Canada.

Library and Archives Canada Cataloguing in Publication

Title: Barangay : an offshore poem / Adrian De Leon ; photographs by Jason Edward Pagaduan.
Names: De Leon, Adrian, author. | Pagaduan, Jason Edward, photographer.
Identifiers: Canadiana 20210253959 | ISBN 9781989496367 (softcover)
Classification: LCC PS8607.E23525 B36 2021 | DDC C811/.6—dc23

To my family

Author's Note

[redacted],
may you read this from the haze.

: a table of contents

barangay, *n.*
a preamble

venus

can a bangka
hold us

when the ocean
stings your limbs?

can these sails
steer us past the breach

when *clotilda* billows
you around like shrouds?

will these outriggers
keep us afloat

when slavers ledger
you as dead weight?

can we cradle skin
against resplendent skin

when guineamen
gut an umbilical past?

will we paddle
ashore

a stolen land?

for the archipelagos

from Kiribati
to Castries

from Luzon
to Lanai

from Ainu Mosir
to Aotearoa

from Tawi-Tawi
to Tonga

from Singapore
to Scarborough

what tempest strands us
on the disappearing shores?

(depuis Édouard Glissant)

in the
salish sea,
our clock   flickers
from   *the wake:*
when a   blaze breaks
the lavender,   we call the embers
morning;   a wrestle between
desperate   ray and
relentless   cloud, we name
their romp   the afternoon; if amber
blinds the   retina, we bid
good night   to the sun; if icc seems
to shimmer   in waves as above,
we greet   the night.
the stern   germinates
into the earth,   branching timelines
like cedars   evergreening into the shore.
can we burn   the water's waxy
leaves into   necessary medicine?
will we breathe   its smoke until our
memory   scars over? or will
our time   be denied
from us   until the shoal
beds   the dead
into the grains   of an hourglass?

An American Delusion

When AMERICA frees you
from Soleimani,
you Saigon jungle people who
scurry
from your boondocks will welcome
the liberators
of Guam from the Spanish clutches
around your
Caribbean island. Rest easy,
little brown brothers,
for AMERICA is here to frack
every ~~gook~~ rallying
from the sand against First Secretary
Hussein – no comrade
of yours. You will shout freedom
from camptowns,
built to protect you from
the Supreme Leader of North
San Salvador, keeping you stale
so you can gather bananas
& maintain our AMERICA abroad
so that one day you can
unearth each of your fingers
to frack that liquid black gift of
freedom.

January 2020

dung-aw

belaboured brothers,

when you hammered
each railroad stake
into the earth,

did you hear them wail
at their reunion
with Shoshone blood?

did the soot
sit unmourned?

did your femurs
rattle the kindred chorus
rearranging bones beneath you?

did you strike
the first notes
of the requiem we call

the Americas?

(to Guangdong brethren at Promontory Point, Utah, 1869)

dung-aw

this mortuary:
marooned
into dewey decimals,

a last glimpse of persons about to disappear into the slave hold.

to these halls'
professional gatekeepers, each body
corresponds to a line in the catalogue,
each rib a folder
among the femurs plundered
from the hoard, what bones wreck
beneath.

spine against spine,
shelved on ancient wood
and guarded marble,

I saw a grave,

but no epitaphs
except ethnologies, no lifespans listed
except the date of acquisition.

here is the shoreline

of the famished cemetery.

here are the waves

of the slaughterhouse.

here are archives

in our stars.

(after Saidiya Hartman)

dung-aw

when did each *now* curl
around the stock exchange
modular arithmetic

when did the cock's crow mark
the morning ritual of whips
the reaping that cracks at dawn

against fleshy gong
grandfathered clock

nine deaths in sixty seconds

twohundredfortynine triggers
seven months

as cyclical as shopping
to bleed as periodic as breath

grief is a strange unending pause

clock   release
each name

clock   around
each rifle's neck

clock   drown
each magazine

(for El Paso, Daytona and lives interrupted)

sky constellates boats,
the fleeting fleshy archipelagos,
brown still flickering
warm with driftwood.
drifters dreamed too of azure
spray- ing penance on their
toes until *đại dương*
fades to navy black.
some
up
crests,
down cradles
cascading the
breach, praying
the saline
sail to safety
hál hañsat. here,
passports ori-
gami island chains
soaked stateless.
the ma-
rooned pilipinas
betrays the
blood scabbing
from urban high-rises
to people under
street
lights,
dreaming *dagat*
churning
pasig river seances for their gone.

barangay, *n.*

[maysa]

ti baranggaymi

our seas

wave

us

ashore

boxes

in algal

shoal

hands

to

home

once, barangay
sighed along
the pasig
where reeds
shook in *the wake.*
where shanty shores
now stilt, whetstoned bolos
waded through bill-
owing fish. once,
pasig churched from
the same gasps that stretched
these sails. once,
mga *tala*
pooled to sweep
us here.

dung-aw

/isa/: a phone call

lola –

into the steinway
of your sala

the way that russian teachers
shoved my hands
into the false ivory?

if you watched
my wrists arch
a "clair de lune"

would you have offered
an alberti bass
to my triads?

might we have scherzoed
a cadence to
disharmony?

your son's arthritic hands?

/dalawa/: beso-beso

bleached &
          leathered forehead

the afterimage
          of cordovilla
sun

          & fold

creasing
          a disenchantment

/tatlo/: archive

then from a fading page –

from jesuit vaults
from filing cabinets

vigil over portraits
dead as you –

baril ng guerilla

ngipin ng hapon

lolo's stories

in typhoon rain

o tal vez

you spoke the scraps

between the cane

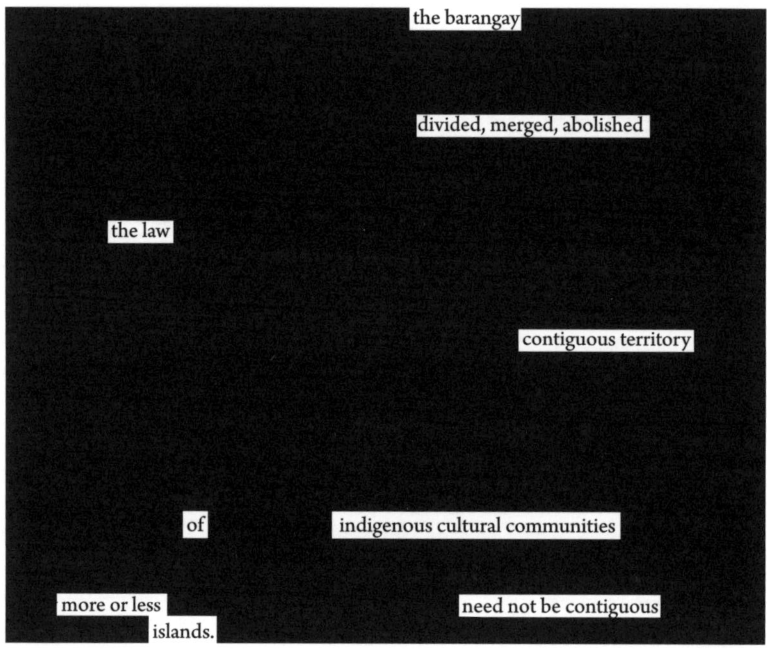

(The local Government Code of the Philippines, Book III, 1991.)

dung-aw

1996

half-bound books
too hefty
for my age
on the makeshift desk –

1997

your simmering
efforts to steep
my skull with a remote
world's necessary skills –

1998

I carried your gift
into flight when the ship
took me up
and lifted an ocean away.

2008

on the telephone
I hear our time together wither
under English's
decrepit weight –

2009

when I visit
your limp gait
or the piecemeal Tagalog
I can't reciprocate –

2012

and now I
blanket again
on the placid place
where the last of you is laid.

(for "Baby" Alcantara, 1940–2012)

barangay, *n.*

[dua]

ti baranggaymi

where island clouds
along a midnight

scatters a wayward library
this boat charts safety
draws a new map

ilog

/isa/: a circumcision

at bedtime my father liked to trace the rush
    of the tenejero river into my homeland dreams

I crouched on the shore & watched the leeches lurch
    the gnawing soil a foot from my not-yet-callused toes

upstream boys bawled at the quack doctor's cleaver
    before he shoved guava leaves into their mouths

magnguya ka   chew until mush   dumura ka sa titi mo

the rouge river has no shamans   not anymore   just urologists
    or whom to play up your pain

binata ka na   di ka na supot
    the boy becomes man
between my legs & asks if adulthood had to hurt

and I spit
    these leaves at the rawness of an unhooded penis

/dalawa/: before the return,

my parents lighted us away to another river

the asphyxiated sun
                                        browned my skin

as the pasig against the ruined

stilts of riverside barangay
                                                    I dreamed

the bubbling waters

the shantytowns into the fjords that lead

to tadoussac
                                  perhaps I'd finally find

the strong winding arms in bataan
            the tenejero

this place could not be home
            until I plunged my waist at the
                                                            depths

the leeches I'd name
            across the ocean

pierced into my flesh to bleed me better
            from the bruise, now mine
                                        of tatay's heels

/tatlo/: the tenejero

at tatay's

leech-filled waters

loved me

in the night

grovelled

through the tar –

the banks revenants

shrieking below

the overpass

without the releases

of meeting its mother sea

bataan, 2009

/apat/: vigil

how do we remember a river buried?

barangay, *n.*

[tallo]

ti baranggaymi

it scalds/the throat
                    ochre/lost to the torso's
acid sea/evidence
                    of debt/of *utang*
it barricades/intoxicates
                    the bank account/screaming
never free

“drowning is the last lullaby of the sea”

virginian icarus
inflated wings
    around your shoulders –

at the wave pool apex
    submerged
    from fullest gasp –

a voice bubbling
    the caesura
    a quiet help –

your treading
    in a water tomb
    only a ripple –

did you fly or breach
    too far
    the flailing white arms?

or did they drown you
    when you dared to claim
    the sterile sea?

(after Craig Santos Perez)

Philippine Studies

On a fresh week for rage, my father scattered
open garbage cans across my bedroom floor.

I had dreamed that I was back in Taguig, sifting through
sheet metal in the alley behind the quail egg stand;

a rusty corrugated corner pierced a bag of rancid chicken
before my eyes stung open from the same stench.

Years before, leather lashed at my flesh & I reveried
bloody-knuckled ways to forgive each crack; instead,

I supposed that it was the rattan of alabaster
nuns beating me through the Father's wrist,

or the hooks whipping welts on the spine of Christ,
raw repentance into clotting, dirt-dyed skin.

When the lashes stopped, new punishments,
creative labours all, sprung from his mind:

guilt-gilded yardwork in the parish I never asked for;
lifelong labour taxes for the upkeep of the pastor indoors;

or this morning, kitchen compost dispersed like us
across my floor: the burden of sensing the homeland.

Later that week, we gathered written scraps of property
around the dining table to stitch into my parents' will.

I inherited his freckles, but couldn't distinguish
which came from Father & which came from Sun.

estuaries

barangay, *n.*

[uppat]

ti baranggaymi

lake air thickens
into darkness

if you grasp
you'll land

if you listen
our oars maroon

the tempest
a thalassocracy

new mother
new tongue

b(rown) c(ommons)

my skin
the river
drags
into the sea

my waist
swells
along
the shore

the bluffs
burn white
the scar

my palms
valley

my toenails
route
returns
in the soil

my body
this earth
alive

(después José Esteban Muñoz)

newborn poem with gasping earth

when you come to,

do you reach
from the static
like cable news?

do you glow
the church
before the dusk
blues the empty pews?

or do you wick
in the breeze
of a last breath?

will your toes
trace a wake
across my palms,

their creases
charting nebulae
into our beyond?

(for L, b. April 2020)

before the cock coaxed iron

cage

our noses prod the gaps for air.
then, mouth on mouth. chalices wet as
christ.

we
momentary
raptures

grope and cave
our late-night cotton like you knuckle

our inner thighs' evidence,
my tongue against
the last drop of you,

bringing white fisher boy

home down the dreaming moon.

your given names

the pink

of your palate –

as devotionals

to a rough sketch

of your rising

the tender bones

against the roundness

you

pantomime –

to its unruliness

and you might speak

for the first time

barangay, *n.*

[lima]

ti baranggaymi –

maris daga masts

hangin
from maynilad

blanket
bluffs

wash away
these nettled
grooves

course salt
into rouge

before that bloody
televised july,
the gravel scraped our knees
still tender from the womb
danzig.
we sunburned into
the ochre pelt of naismiths.
we bounced
until our bellies swelled, aching
from the searing chicken
grease.
every melted jos louis,
every fanta pop we shared,
robin hoods gallivanting from
the blue.

tungtungan

after David Chariandy

> The Rouge Valley. It was a wound in the earth. A scar of green running through our neighbourhood, hundreds of feet deep in some places, a glacial valley that existed long before anything called Scarborough.
>
> – *Brother*

<u>ACT I</u>

<u>SCENE 1</u>

(look down the bluffs)

(BLACKOUT)

(END OF SCENE)

SCENE 2

(walk south)

hike where morningside ends:
my calves accustomed to the minute
distances of barangay alleys
when I hoist myself
over the metal barrier.

(at the offending object, a
hardy bolt head)

I hid my limp behind my corduroy,
corrugated leggings concealing a cut
landscape
sutured by orton park bridge.

(END OF SCENE)

SCENE 3

winding into the birch
called us itself.
in manila, our barangay arches
greened with oxidation.
here, the ravine sighs
in midsummer.

(shuts teeth)

my father, boy of bataan
hikes ahead of his laggard son,
marches years ahead
of the heart attack to come.

(END OF SCENE)

SCENE 4

(to camera)

My parents miss the sea.
Hell, we picnic at the bluffs for days, it
seems.
This soy sauce we're baptized in daily salts
the shores of Bataan in our mouths.
Tatay speaks the Lake Ontario gust
and a dirge away a thought forms his saline
childhood again. Mariveles, you could say,
as Tatay's river.

Nanay holds the bangus fish
by its belly and its back crisp
as a rubber band caught too long against a
thumb,
releases the pasig of her mother's looking
back.

(END OF SCENE)

SCENE 5

(over the edge)

I don't remember how we climbed back up;

my limp buckled somewhere
north of Dubarry Avenue.

In the sputtering silence
of our basement:
a bottle of Neosporin;
my glistening knee.

(END OF SCENE)

<u>SCENE 6</u>

the gate, once spread,
now reveals a remnant path
behind the brush that drops off early.

and storms that bruise
the Bluffs' faces
wince from gashes, scabs
churning foam below.

we climb the Bluffs now
with our Best Buy eyes,
high above our viewfinders.

(END OF SCENE)

SCENE 7

Sixteen years after that picnic,
a trout hurries past my eyes.

It sketches sinusoidal paths
into the river, leaps for knolls
over its sidewalk cracks,
hikes down its own Morningside,
makes believe an ocean
at the end of this road.

(END OF SCENE)

kundiman

tugang:

at victoria park I watched you
erupt above the surface
hardening into an island

in honolulu, you found savai'i
and the nihon you never thought
you'd hear from beyond the dead

when the seabed
grabbed your ankles
you let it wash you west

you'd fall in love with edsa
the slow grey currents
that carry the city around
like river sludge

or you'd meet our mother
mountain once a perfect cone
the smoking pencil scribbling
native tales into the sky

tugang:

when you see this poem
maybe manila's screeching steel
could by instinct fill your lungs
with midland air

or maybe you might rustle
in the fallen malunggay

make-believing
the oak and birch
of home
            though incomplete
                        like love

(for Patrick, at Wai'alae)

barangay, n.

[innem]*

ti baranggaymi –
agsao ken da ubbing
ni amianan ken da kordilyera,
ni Cagayan ken 'diay Isabela,
maka-awatanmi
dagiti bakras
sadinno makasinnabatkami.

tributaries

On *barangay*

At once maritime and landlocked. The eighth sea and the one hundred eleventh cell. The outrigger balanced us on each side, waves where Fujian fingers and sea cucumbers meet. Where vagrant royals reap the spoils of native shame. Where sway the ghosts of Spanish sails, before they anchored us to the dirt. To cathedral bells that rang savage once we stepped too far from Catholic songs. An outrigger boat. A neighbourhood. Something umbilical in an age of fracture.

On Some Poetic Forms in this Book

Luzon's submerged north. Southward in Manila Bay, *mahal* meant love, but also head tax. Mahal, expensive. On dung-aw, *recuerdos de patay* petrified the rigor mortis and emulsion from the camera's spine. Like Ate's shell of Lola Fanny when I got the news of her death. The boats and shapes harbour a homecoming, wherever we go. Love. Mourning chants. Barangay

On Denial

For you, translation is my gift. I edge you to meaning, perch you against the rumbling waterfall with the patience of my tongue, string your moaning *por favor.* I cuff your wrists from the dictionary's aid. If not my mouth. Just the page into your ear until you come upon it dazzling.

On Spanish

The rhotic flaps the sides of my tongue. Uvula into the desired trill, but still too dulcet for the peninsula's *mandatos.* To the front of the picket lines, wave its signs. It hesitates, ashamed that I would push the wind – *hangin* – from my diaphragm. Indio followed my melanin like a poltergeist. These sounds were meant to conquer. Me? *Cada palabra en este idioma será mi Reconquista.*

On Tagalog

From the west, it felt *matigas* as throbbing cock behind the Value Village. From Luzon's north, its hands Scarborough schools, the cure for a scratchy throat pinned down with Popsicle stick: ESL. From home, it whipped and cooked and prayed and kissed and moved until *hiya:* shame.

On Ilokano

Two by two, from the bottom bunk of Lola's room when José's *maris daga* scattered as dust she and Nanay wept in a language that should have been my own. At the dinner table, they yielded to the sounds of imperial Manila. In Mānoa concrete, between the Maunakea Market stalls, that darker speech, once buried, clawed from my throat. It lived in me from that first visit home. It crescendoes with the brief scrawls of the *tungtungan* worlded in these poems.

On Tanyag

My Manila outrigger, the sea of smog. Translates to "popular," a bangka for Southern Ilokanos only. Waist-high me haunts the grey between the shanty coves. Lola's brother built that hut to set our family sail. A lifeline from Pasay to the sputtering barangay at the base of the Cordillera. Lola spoke of province days like faded tapestry. My callused toes recall the frantic pedalling past the jeepneys during rush hour sludge. Tito Alan scooped me from the doom. Fire ants gnawed at my heels, eager for the snack of Catholic guilt. The dread of authority flying home from Arabian petroleum. Dito na si Tatay mo, anak.

On Scarborough

We blackened, browned and yellowed valleys not our own. We mushroomed spores dispersed from patria to pools of blood that mingle native land. Kneading, stir-frying, pickling homelands into life. Matsutakes in the clearing of Toronto's shrapnel. While mouths that cut their teeth on self-professing expertise scavenge between our fingers. Insurgency. Stealing stories on leathered skin.

On Rouge (River) and Ganatsekwyagon

Double-decker trains wail their lime-green nightmares. Turtle Island geese. Tank tops and Air Force Ones long beneath umbrellas and clean water certification. Upstream, summer reeds carrying place had portaged farther north. The Confederacy paddled upstream in ways a barangay might understand.

On *Rouge*

Agbibiag, ay-ayaten, ken aglalaay ni Lelangko kadagiti tallo a lengguahe. Arapaapek para ti bigat inton-ano makasuratko para isuna kenni inauna a lengguahena, Ilokano. The pledge incomplete like subway lines – the first book – in Brown neighbourhoods, I spent this volume suturing with my pen. Scabs like autumn auburn. Wound in the earth. Kayumanggi. Chicken pox phantoms constellate freckles on my face. "My grandmother lives, loves and grieves in three languages. I dream of the day when I can write in her most native Ilokano."

[**six**]*

our barangay –
speak with the children
the north and the mountains,
Cagayan and Isabela,
understand
the slopes
where we all can meet.

**a translation*

Legend*

barangay:	a pre-colonial Philippine outrigger boat (also called a bangka) the basic unit of Philippine social life
dung-aw:	mourning chants
ilog:	river
kayumanggi:	brown
kundiman:	love songs
[maysa] | /isa/ [dua] | /dalawa/ [tallo] | /tatlo/ [apat] | /uppat/ [lima] | /lima/ etc.	one two three four five
niigani-gichigami	leading sea, Scarborough's shore
ti baranggaymi	our barangay
tugang	brother
tungtungan:	story

**for the time being*

Acknowledgements

This book wasn't supposed to happen. An archival trip while editing *Rouge*, my first book and last one until grad school was done, and a grandmother dies. A picture of her body sent to me. A friend told me to write. And keep writing. In whatever language it came out, to mourn and "write in the language of the diaspora." So, I wrote in Toronto, and rewrote in Los Angeles, and rewrote again in a pandemic, and in the process, built this blueprint of a boat you now hold in your hands.

My gratitude to Canisia Lubrin, who pulled this book from the doldrums. Thank you for your faith in the promise of this work. You were the Virgil to take this – and me – out of the inferno through your editorial magic. Thanks also to the Wolsak & Wynn team, for giving this little book the love it deserves.

To everyone who builds this boat with me:

Listeners in Toronto, Los Angeles and Vancouver.

Everywhere and anywhere –
Christine. Jonathan. Samphoas. Jason. Wes. Gym. Jojo. Chloe.

USC –
ASE colleagues, especially Sonia, Kitty, Jujuana, Viet, Dorinne, John, Nayan, Oneka, Shawn, Eddie. Marlon. Alaina. Reaghan. Deena. Layla. Angela. Ana. AnnaBella. Jennifer. Jordan. Tiffany. Dylan. Kiana. Ananya. Faith. Prim. Hunter. Bao. Bo. Gemma. Megan. Jerald. Courtney. All of you, for your compassion.

Seattle and in between –
Roneva. Madison. Anna. Jorge. Vince. Nikhil. Marlena. Janna. Kendra. Aunties and uncles. Anna. Gary. Gilda. Pete. Dorothy. Fred, from the beyond. The Manangs and Manongs.

Los Angeles –
Tita and my cousins. Dada. Oona. Royce. Kierra. Liz. Dolly. Sulafa.

Toronto –
Tak. Lisa. Kevin. Robert. Bonnie. Amela. Lily. Minying. Niyosha. Julian. Michael. Brenton. Chris. Anthony. Dina. Claire. Ariana. Delila. Helen, in your memory. Phil. Ying.

Scarborough –
Daniel. Carrianne. Catherine. David. Noor. Téa. Jason, for your vision. Patrick. Diriye. Yusef. Hassan. Natasha. Daniela.

barangay –
My kuntaw family. Lola. Ate. Kuya. Pat. Paul. Leanna. Titos and titas. Nanay. Tatay. Anders.

And to you, dear reader, for setting sail with me.

Adrian De Leon is a writer and educator from Manila by way of Scarborough, Ontario. He is the author of *Rouge* (2018) and co-editor of *FEEL WAYS: A Scarborough Anthology* (2021), both published by Mawenzi House. His poetry and nonfiction have appeared in *The Puritan*, *Joyland Magazine*, *Asian American Writers' Workshop* and *Catapult*. His research has been featured in *VICE*, the *Los Angeles Times*, *National Geographic*, ABC *Nightline*, *The Guardian* and *Rolling Stone*. Adrian currently lives in Los Angeles, where he is an Assistant Professor of American Studies and Ethnicity at the University of Southern California.